From Whom Much Is Given...

Antoine Carey

From Whom Much Is Given… by *Antoine Carey*
Published by *ThroneRoom Expressions*
ThroneRoom Expressions Publishing Headquarters
33 Old Mill Lane
Southampton, PA 18966

©2022 Antoine Carey.. All rights reserved. No part of this publication may be reproduced, stored in a retrieval system or transmitted in any form by any means, mechanical, electronic, photocopying, recording or otherwise – without the prior written permission of the author.

Cover Design by *ThroneRoom Expressions* & *Addison Graphics*
Editing by *ThroneRoom Expressions.*

For more information please contact:
ThroneRoom Expressions Publishing
throneroomexpressions@gmail.com.
info@charphelpsinternational.com
www.charphelpsinternational.com

Library of Congress Control Number: *2022934792*

Printed in the United States

DEDICATION

All praise be to Allah, the Creator and Sustainer of all that exists.

CONTENTS

Introduction ………………………………………..5

Fade in Full - "The Story of Antoine Carey"
    Transcribed ……………………………...7

Chapter 1: Same Thing That Make
    You Laugh, Make You Cry …………………21

Chapter 2: Where There's A Will,
    There's A Way……………………………..26

Chapter 3: When The Good You Do,
    Don't Do You No Good ………………..44

Chapter 4: The More Things Change,
    The More They Remain the Same …………....56

Chapter 5: If It Don't Cost You Anything,
    It's Not Worth Anything ……………….65

Chapter 6: He Who Is Closest To The
    Problem Is Closet To The Solution……………69

Chapter 7: Many Hands Make Light Work …………...75

INTRODUCTION

Fade in Full "The Story of Antoine Carey" debuted at the Marquee Cinemas – Southpoint in Fredericksburg, Virginia on February 24, 2019; exactly five years to the day of my release from the Virginia Department of Corrections. The documentary depicts my life from childhood through years in prison to the present-day entrepreneur and public speaker that works with local organizations to help at-risk youth break generational cycles of incarceration. The film was birthed by the notion that we have experiences in our lives that are not necessarily for us as much as it may be for the benefits of others.

Given the fact that we all have a story and the propensity to positively impact those around us, I feel it's a moral obligation to share our stories. I'm blessed that others have been receptive to my story and found it to be a source of inspiration. It's in this same spirit I endeavor to continue sharing my experiences in hopes they do not return void. It is my most earnest prayer that through transparency and full disclosure I'm able to restore hope in the lives of those affected by incarceration, combat recidivism and be a voice for the voiceless.

It's important to note at this time that I do not have all the answers. I am only Antoine and merely speak from my thirty-eight years of experience. I've made enough mistakes and bad decisions for two lifetimes and if I'm blessed to live long enough, I'm destined to make plenty more. It's with this I apologize in advance. Anything I may say that is right and exact I credit to Allah. Anything I say that may misguide anyone is due to my own lower self. Secondly, my most important disclaimer is that neither this book nor any of its contents is intended to negate or justify me taking full responsibility for all of my actions and subsequent consequences. If we are to ever change our circumstances, we must first change ourselves and that begins with accountability.

With that being said, this book is based on actual events. The story you are about to read is real. These are not characters. No name of any person or place has been changed to protect identities. This is "From Whom Much Is Given…."

-Antoine Carey

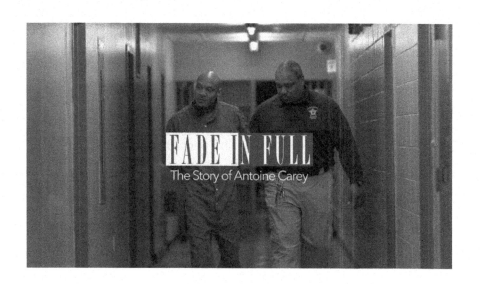

FADE IN FULL
"THE STORY OF ANTOINE CAREY"
TRANSCRIBED

(INTRO NARRATED BY ANTOINE CAREY)

It actually was my 22nd birthday and I always keep it in my head like Catch 22, I got caught at 22. I sparked a jay and I hit it two times. I give it to him and he hit the blunt two times. I see blue lights behind us. He like, "Yo, that's the police." He asked me, "Are they on us?" and I say, "Yeah bro, they on us." I already got a .45 that's laid in the floorboard of the car. A month earlier I had been arrested in Norfolk for having a concealed weapon. I don't have any felony convictions at this time, but I still had this firearm that's in the car. He comes to the car, I give him my license and registration and I inform him that there is a gun in the car. He takes the gun. He takes the clip out of it and set it on the hood of the car. For his protection he asked me to step out of the vehicle then he puts me in handcuffs and lets me know I'm not under arrest; it's just for his safety. I explained to him it was my birthday. I was smoking which is a misdemeanor.

> He was like, "I'm going to call the gun in and if everything is registered, I'll write you a citation and you'll be on your way."

Now I'm clean but as they're searching him a bag of coke falls out of his pocket. They take me and put me in the backseat of the police car and I am watching as they're searching the vehicle. Now I know in the trunk I have four and a half ounces of coke and two sawed-off shotguns. I see him take the key out the ignition and walk around to the back of the trunk. When he goes and he starts jingling [the keys] all I could do was fall and lay my head over in the floorboard of the car because I know it's about to go bad from here.

Antoine Carey: My name is Antoine Carey. I grew up in Center Cross, Virginia. A point of reference would be Tappahannock, Virginia. I had a normal childhood. I grew up in a divorced family which my father wasn't in the home but he was in the area and very active in my life. I have a twin sister and two elder sisters. Because I grew up in a household with just my sisters, I tended to try and blend in with other families that had males. I didn't come from a bad family. We weren't rich. I never went without anything. I was never faced with a lot of the ills that other families may have been faced with. I don't remember the electricity being cut off or not having water in the house.

Ms. Martha Carey: I did the best I could.

Antoine Carey: You did, you did a great job!

Ms. Martha Carey: I got out here and worked two jobs to give y'all what other kids had and I did that too. Y'all did good. I had smart kids, you know.

Antoine Carey: My sisters they kind of paved the way for what was to be expected of me because I was the baby of the family. That's one of the things that I really can't piece together. I didn't grow up in the city. There were no tall buildings. There were no projects. There wasn't a lot of crime. When I would go to Richmond or cities or places with tall buildings and projects, it was like I wish that I had grown up there. Little did I know, I really didn't know the ins and outs of the cities. There was some familiarity there even though I hadn't grown up there. I believe I was maybe fifteen years old when I had my real first brush with the law or real trouble. It was a possession of marijuana at Essex High School. It was a small slap on the wrist. It was like okay; I can stand a little bit of trouble and it really wasn't that bad.

I ended up at Norfolk State University and I was smoking a whole lot of weed at that time. There was a Jamaican cat that stayed right off of the side of campus. Naturally, he ran a 24-hour weed spot and after a while of building a rapport with him he asked me if I ever dabbled in cocaine. I had seen coke before, but I had never sold it. The numbers were great. The coke was amazing. He broke me off like two ounces and a quarter or six deuce is what they called it. He dropped that on me and told me to take that up the road and see what I could do with it.

By the time I got up the road and actually had someone to put it together or cook it rather, like it was that. That is how I acquired the name *"College Boy."* My mother and my father stayed right there in Center Cross where I would move around at. To elude them, they couldn't call and say that Antoine was up the road. They would say *College Boy* and that name always stuck with me. I received a year-and-a-half sentence for my first possession with intent to distribute and possession of a firearm, and other drug charges. I did receive a bond at that time when I caught those charges. Meanwhile, I had been made aware my daughter's mother was in fact pregnant.

During that time, before going back to court my father passed that September. My last incarceration was really an eye-opener because I was facing real time. The plea they offered was for some serious time but the severity of the situation hadn't clicked yet. The original charges were attempted second degree murder, possession of a firearm by a felon, shooting into an occupied dwelling and use of a firearm in commission of a felony. Just on paper reading these, several of these charges carried mandatory minimum sentences.

I figured if I could just get work release and get a job set up, I could stay at the regional jail. Little did I know I was going to prison. I was going up the road this time. When we went to sentencing that day, the sentencing guidelines was two years to two years and four months. So, I'm thinking four years maybe three years and some change then I'll be home. My son was born on a Friday and I had to turn myself in for these charges on a Wednesday. I'm still thinking I'm going to be there to watch him grow up. The judge came back and I remember his words, "It is better to have never had then to have and had squandered, and you Mr. Carey are the latter." He sentenced me to seventeen years with five suspended leaving me a twelve-year active sentence on top of the year and a month sentence I had in Essex at the time.

So, it was like you just gave me twelve years that didn't even start until next October. I remember him reading the charges off and the first one was shooting into an occupied dwelling – ten years with two years suspended. I remembered hearing him but, in my mind, I was playing back I know he didn't just give me eight years especially when I know he got three more charges to read off. I could hear my sisters and my cousin screaming in the background as he was reading those charges off. It's still not resonating with me what's going on. All I could do was look back over my shoulder and say, "It's alright, we alright."

I was sentenced like on a Wednesday. That following Monday they tapped my bunk, "Carey B&B," and I was like what's going on. I'm still trying to get in contact with my lawyer and appeal my case. They were like "Nah, you going to prison this morning." I had dreads all the way down my back. They take me out the pod and get me to booking and I remember asking one of the CO's that was cool. She said, "You know they going to cut those dreads off your head as soon as you get there" and I was like "Man they not cutting my hair." She was like "You are going and if you don't cut it you going to the hole." I remember asking her "Is it alright if you allow me to cut my dreads here?" and she did. So, I remember being shackled up with my hands, I cut all my dreads off and left it in property. I remember being on the Department of Corrections bus on the way to prison that morning shackled down, shaking my head and my dreads weren't moving. It's like yo this is really happening. Sitting inside of a prison cell you're forced to accept who you are and who you are not.

I was still College Boy, but I was College Boy without dreads. I was still College Boy but now I'm waiting on a money order and I don't have access to my own money. I was still College Boy but I didn't have any females writing me or coming to visit me. Everything that I thought was cool to be able to come home and say I did, time was like okay well now you're doing time. One of the tattoos I got when I was locked up was "Everybody want to go to heaven but nobody want to die." Dudes want to say you got this rep or you are this type of person, but it cost to do those things.

This wasn't a price I wanted to pay. Again, it never really resonated with me that I was going to do all this time. That was kind of my defense mechanism. I never really truly accepted that this was real. Some would equate being in prison to being buried alive. I've never hurt so much in forcing myself to accept who I was and who I wasn't. You're not this tough guy. You do hurt, you do cry, you're Antoine and there's nothing wrong with being Antoine. I had to redefine who I was so I could attract those things that I wanted out of life but I know that this wasn't it.

I went to the law library regularly and read about not only the elements that need to be present, but I was also able to study the sentencing that was in correlation with those elements in those specific crimes. I didn't necessarily meet all of those requirements to be convicted of those said crimes. I was able to forward this information along to my attorney Michael Morchower at the time. Also, I was able to come to the realization that a lot of crimes wasn't so black and white. It was a lot of gray areas where a lot of guys fell victim to circumstances that qualified them for particular crimes. [Graphic: In America 2.2 million incarcerated] which is a 400% increase from 40 years ago. I figured that this was due to there was more violent criminals or more crimes being committed.

The reality is that it's due to the change in law and policy. So, you had individuals who are sentenced to lengthy sentences but went up for parole ever so often, had good behavior and then was released. Well, in 1995 parole was abolished. So, when I come along, I received a sentence expected to serve 85% of that sentence before I'm even eligible for any type of release. Now the laws and policy have changed again because so many of my generation have been released and reconvicted. Now they have mandatory minimum sentences, in which case, regardless of the circumstances of your crimes and conviction for these charges you have a mandatory sentence.

There is no longer any consideration given to the individual as more is placed on the actual crime itself. I was originally charged with attempted second-degree murder which was amended down to attempted *unlawful* wounding. I was also convicted of *malicious* shooting within an occupied dwelling which in essence, is a conflict of charges. Therefore, (by way of habeas corpus) I was able to give back eight years of the sentence, in which I was sentenced to ten years with two suspended for the malicious shooting within a building. They suspended or dismissed the malicious shooting within an occupied dwelling. My original sentence was thirteen years, eight of which was for the conviction of malicious shooting within an occupied dwelling. Once that charge was dismissed, I was released eight years earlier.

Faded & Company came to me as I was sitting in the first barber shop I worked at upon coming home and that was Kingdom Cuts in downtown Fredericksburg. I was hired on as a licensed barber in which case, a licensed barber is not an employee as much as it is an independent contractor. So, upon being given this opportunity I was given the key to the shop. I was sitting there one day and I was like I'm building a little clientele and I wanted to be able to have something like this of my own. The name *"Faded"* is more of an urban term. Urban guys you know we get a fade so faded pun intended. The *"and Company"* is because I wanted to also have a distinguished look on paper and that was where the *"and Company"* came in. *Faded & Company* or the barbershop rather for me, has always been a focal point of the community.

I like to think that when I draped a client up I had them for at least 45 minutes. It gave me an opportunity to share my story and not just to take hair off their head but also to pour something into them while I had them there with me. I met Mrs. Juanita at a Department of Corrections re-entry Summit that I was asked to speak at alongside

Harold Clark which is director of the Department of Corrections.

Mrs. Juanita Shanks: When I heard him speak, I saw that he had potential to make a difference in others' lives. My name is Juanita Shanks, and I am the President and CEO of Failsafe Era. Failsafe Era is a 501(c)3 nonprofit organization that works with individuals affected by incarceration. That means the inmates, the returning citizens, and the family members. So, I just wanted to work with him and just kind of help him move in the direction that he wanted to go in, to help him get to his destiny. As we walked through this process [actually with my son] is when I really recognized the importance of helping to remove those barriers for individuals who had been affected by incarceration. So, for us it is important to change the lives of individuals that have been affected by incarceration, to help rebuild our communities and to help those family members to understand that life is not over and there is still hope for their future.

Antoine Carey: I felt that it was an honor that she would look at me in such a light that she was willing to invest into me. One of the greatest blessings I feel Faded and Company has afforded Antoine the man, is the ability to not only pour into young men here in the barbershop but to have an invitation extended to me to appear at numerous High Schools in the community. I was given the opportunity to speak to some students at Massaponax high school today and share a little bit of my story in hopes that the mistakes I made will prevent them from making the same. I feel it is of the utmost importance to be proactive vs. reactive in our endeavor of saving these young men's lives not only from incarceration but consequences of bad decisions. I pray that I am afforded more opportunities in order to reach out and impact more lives not only here in the local community but abroad. I feel we have a social responsibility especially within the community to not only be in the community, but to be a part of the community which gives us an opportunity to build those relationships. We are able to meet other organizations that are invested into pouring back into the community. Each event that we have attended we've met other people who have other organizations or counsels that are already organizing other things that they are inviting us to. A lot of times they say it takes a village. I think the more that we are seen and the more exposure we have it opens up the door for the story to be told more often.

Mrs. Juanita Shanks:: He is doing it out of his heart. He is doing it because he cares. It makes me feel good to know that someone that at one point took from our community is now giving back and giving it back to the youth especially.

Antoine Carey: Given my story, given the fact that I am in fact guilty of those charges that I was convicted and sentenced for, given the many men that I've come across while fighting for my freedom that are yet to obtain theirs with even more valid reasons for them to be home. Given the platform that I've been afforded to be put in front of people's kids some of their most prized possessions and to speak to one barber that has a life sentence that so happened to be one of my barber aides while I went through the class and for him to share with me how he lives through me because he may never get this chance.

Mrs. Juanita Shanks: The things that I have seen Antoine do. The way in how he relates to other youth and how he is being such an example and role model for his son and his daughter. He is making such an impact in our communities. I'm proud, he makes me very, very proud of him.

Ms. Martha Carey: I talked to a teacher of yours once and she always told me don't ever forget Antoine is talented and I told her that the other day. I said he is doing a good job, you know.

Antoine Carey: Some of us are just slow learners, it takes a little while longer for some of us.

Ms. Martha Carey: Just continue to do good, you know. Antoine put me through so much you just don't know. Money spent and everything, but people change. You are doing good so continue.

Antoine Carey: I've seen young men that enter prison at an age that they were never able to be a man. I see so many that are headed in that direction. I almost feel like that this is my purpose in hopes that if there is only one that I can reach that will allow them to avoid some of the pitfalls that I fell into, that it's worth it.

CHAPTER I
Same Thing That Make You Laugh, Make You Cry

There I was at the pinnacle of my success since being released from prison. The red-carpet premiere of the self-entitled documentary was a huge success and had just weeks earlier been highlighted in a front-page newspaper article in the Free Lance Star. I had earned my barber's license while incarcerated and was able to come home and establish my own barbershop, *Faded & Co.* which was flourishing in its third year of operation.

My story of redemption was constantly being recognized and thus had afforded me the respect of people in the community. I was blessed with opportunities to partner with reputable local organizations including FailSafe - Era, Teen Enrichment Network, Thurman Brisben Shelter and Micah Ministries. During this time, I was regularly invited to speak to the youth at all the high schools in the Spotsylvania and Fredericksburg area. In addition, I had also been the guest speaker at Haynesville Correctional Center, Rappahannock Juvenile Detention Center, and alongside Harold Clark, the Director of the Virginia Department of Corrections at the Northern Neck Reentry Summit. Most importantly, my greatest accomplishment in my personal life at that time was having been awarded full custody of my son, Silas Amir Carey.

It was the evening of April 7th, 2019. Silas and I was attending a family function at a clients' residence. As night began to fall, we headed home so that I could prepare him for school the following morning. While traveling we were passed by a Ford F150 pick-up truck with loud exhaust pipes. My son half-hanging out the window in amazement screams, "Dad that truck is super-fast!" I explain to him that we were riding in a Jaguar which is not only a luxury car but also twice as fast as that truck. To demonstrate I accelerated in an attempt to catch up with the truck. As we approached the intersection, I initiated a right turn but was going too fast. The car began to fish-tail and I over corrected. As a result, the car did a complete 180-degree spin and crashed into the driver's side of a vehicle at the traffic light awaiting to turn left in the direction from which we came.

At the moment of impact, I was immediately consumed with fear and reacted out of impulse. I shifted the car back into drive, did a U-turn in the middle of the road and sped away from the scene of the accident. I drove to my residence and switched vehicles into my Honda Accord. As I was leaving my house all I could think was I didn't want my son to see me get arrested so I headed towards my ex-wife house to drop him off. About ten minutes after leaving my ex-wife's house I received a call from her stating that several Virginia State Troopers were there asking for my whereabouts. Ironically, my car had been identified by the license plate that read "FADED" representing my barbershop's brand name.

    Early the next morning I contacted the Virginia State Police by phone. I was advised that the trooper who was investigating the accident was out of town and asked to meet him the following Wednesday at the Rappahannock Regional Jail. Upon meeting the officer, I was arrested and charged with Felony Leaving the Scene of an Accident, Felony Child Abuse/Neglect and Misdemeanor Reckless Driving. My bond was set at $3,000 and I was released pending my trial date.

    Since my release from prison, I had prided myself on being a rehabilitated man and law-abiding productive citizen. I had taken all the necessary precautions and made all the proper changes. I was intentional in refraining from those behaviors that would potentially jeopardize my freedom. I had successfully detached from those people, places and things that I once identified with that previously led to my incarceration. I was able to surround myself with positive influences and a strong support system. I was diligent to obey all federal, state and local laws.

Due to my felony convictions, I did not use, possess, transport or carry any firearms. I did not unlawfully use, possess, or distribute any controlled substances nor associate with those who did. My transformation had been recognized by the community in which my professional time was contributed and most importantly, by my family with whom I spent my leisure. I had assumed the role as an example to others about making the right decisions and yet here I was, victim to the very same circumstances that I endeavor so hard to combat. Needless to say, I was devastated. I couldn't help but feel that I had failed all those whom I had once inspired. I was consumed with self-doubt as I slipped into a state of depression. I began to question my message, my efforts, and ultimately myself.

CHAPTER 2
Where There's A Will, There's A Way

It was during this pivotal time I remember watching an episode of *Ted Talk* featuring Simon Sinek entitled *"Find Your Why."* I highly recommend that you watch the video in its entirety in order to fully understand his viewpoint. However, for the purpose of this book I will be paraphrasing and sharing what spoke to me in his message. In the clip he explains how successful people tend to focus on their WHY as opposed to their WHAT and HOW. In short, WHAT someone does and HOW it's done fails in comparison to the WHY someone does what they do.

This observation had such a profound impact on me that I often reference it in my speaking engagements using my own examples. To illustrate I draw attention to the recent rivalry between fast-food chains Chick-Fil-A and Popeye's. The two restaurants were publicized last year when the Chick-Fil-A chicken sandwich vs. the Popeye's chicken sandwich comparison went viral. While the craze spiked revenue, it also plagued both companies with grid locked drive-thrus, sold-out featured items, as well as assaults on customers and staff. I was less enthused by the battered chicken cutlet as I was the business' bottom line.

Upon further investigation I uncovered that Popeye's reported annual earnings of $4.4 billion that year. Conversely, Chick-Fil-A which surprisingly has fewer locations and is only open six days a week grossed a staggering $14.2 billion in the same year. How was this possible?

When applying Simon Sinek's theory, we examine the WHAT, HOW and the WHY of both companies. WHAT does both restaurants do? They both merely sell chicken. HOW do they sell chicken? They both implore different recipes, feature items, marketing techniques, etc. in an effort to do what they do and that's sell chicken. It's when we focus on their WHY that we expose the distinction between the two. Popeye's mission statement is, *"To increase franchise success in every facet of the business."* Meanwhile Chick-Fil-A's vision is, *"To glorify God by being a faithful steward of all that is entrusted to us. To have a positive influence on all who come in contact with Chick-Fil-A."*

This is evident in Chick-Fil-A being known for their religious affiliation and impeccable customer service aside from them offering a great chicken sandwich. From this we can conclude that there is more value in WHY we do something compared to WHAT we do and HOW it is done. Also, we can deduce that our WHY remains constant even when our WHAT and HOW is altered.

In my case, WHAT I wanted to do was to have a positive impact on my community. HOW I intended to do this was via barbering and/or public speaking. Now that my WHAT and HOW were affected because of pending charges I was forced to self-evaluate. I began to question my WHY! My WHY was deeply rooted in my desire to share my experiences in order to build relationships in an effort to break cycles of incarceration. I feel an obligation to prevent others from going through what I've been through regardless of if it is accomplished behind a barber chair or behind a microphone.

If my life up to this point had been a source of inspiration and others were able to draw strength from it, then I must continue sharing. I refused to abandon my WHY in spite of the effect my current charges may have on my WHAT and HOW. It was then I decided to exhaust all the WHAT's and HOW's afforded to me as long as I remained true to my WHY. I vowed to be transparent with all the organizations I partnered with and to fully disclose my situation to those inviting me to speaking engagements. I refused to allow this isolated incident to silence my WHY!

I endeavored to overcome this life-altering decision by using this setback as a driving force to foster positive change in the community. Using my barbershop, *Faded & Co.* as a vehicle, we were able to regularly provide the less fortunate with self-respect and dignity in regard to their appearance through free haircuts at the *Thurman Brisben* homeless shelter and *Micah Ministries*. We also extended our services free of charge to foster children for their duration of time in foster care as well as to local youth annually during back-to-school season. I was continually blessed with opportunities to empower and restore hope in the community through public speaking. I was honored to be the guest speaker at the Essex High School Class of 2019 Baccalaureate Ceremony, St. Brides Correctional Center Class of 2019 Graduation and the Virginia Rules Camp sponsored by the Office of the Attorney General.

In addition to the numerous community service events and speaking engagements, I wanted to make more of a lasting impact by offering others the same opportunities I had been afforded. I understood from the relationships I had formed within the community that people were not only in need of inspiration but also an alternative path out of poverty into economic independence. Having faced the stigma of having a past, my goal was to provide training and career opportunities to those with barriers to employment such as past convictions, substance abuse, and domestic violence. I was able to partner with the *Virginia Initiative for Education and Work (VIEW)* program through Spotsylvania Department of Social Services and the *Workforce Innovation Opportunity Act (WIOA)* through Virginia Career Works. My dream came to fruition when *Faded & Co. Barber Academy* was established and blessed to welcome its first class of students in July 2020.

Carey speaks at St. Brides Correctional Center Class of 2019 Graduation

Carey speaks at Fredericksburg Department of Social Services

Carey at Virginia Rules Camp hosted by the Office of the Attorney General

Carey delivered the address at the Baccalaureate service for the 2019 graduates of Essex High School

Carey with students at James Monroe High School

Carey with students at Massaponax High School

Carey provides free haircuts at Thurman Brisben Center

Carey speaks at the Eastern Region Unit Heads meeting hosted by Haynesville Correctional Center

Carey speaks at the Positive Men of Influence Event hosted by UnMasked

Carey speaks at Riverbend High School

Carey appears on the front page of Returning Citizens Magazine

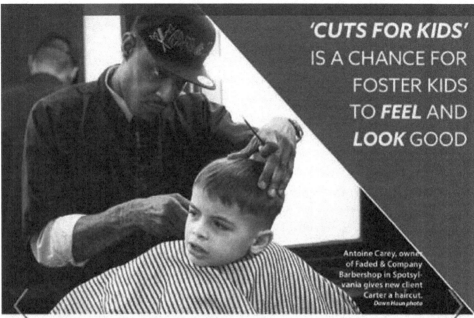

'CUTS FOR KIDS' IS A CHANCE FOR FOSTER KIDS TO *FEEL* AND *LOOK* GOOD

Antoine Carey, owner of Faded & Company Barbershop in Spotsylvania gives new client Carter a haircut.
Dawn Haun photo

Local Barber donates haircuts to foster care kids

By Ann Marie Washington

Imagine not ever going to a barber or salon to get a professional haircut or feel the wow-factor after a 'hair makeover.' So often we take this service for granted, but this is reality for children in foster care.

Gretchen Rusden, recruitment coordinator of Embrace Treatment Foster Care knows all too well of the children's lack of hair care and hygiene. "There are many times when children come into foster care and we are unable to get a comb through their hair," says Rusden.

Earlier this year, Rusden attended the ribbon cutting at the new location for Faded & Company Barbershop. She approached the shop owner Antoine Carey about the need for foster kid's haircuts.

Carey generously jumped at the chance to use his haircutting skills for the kids and create a trusting bond. "To whom much is given, much is required," he recited a quote from the Bible. "We are blessed with talents, wealth, knowledge, and time, in the community and I can give back to benefit others."

One of Carey's new foster care clients, Carter, came by for a haircut with his foster parents before they headed out to an Easter egg hunt. As Carter sat in a booster seat on top of the barber chair, he was more interested in the cartoons on the TV than the sound of the razor humming as Carey carefully trimmed the hair around his ears. Afterwards, he jumped down from the chair, stared in the mirror, smiled and gave Carey a 'high-five.'

Rusden spoke of how much this service is needed- not only for the hygiene, but how it impacts the foster child's

Continued on page 24

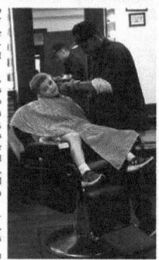

Carey provides free haircuts at Embrace Treatment Foster Care

Faded & Co. Annual
Fade Into Summer
Community Day of Service

Carey with students at James Monroe High School

Carey with Faded & Co. Barber Shop staff

Carey with Faded & Co. Barber Academy students

Carey featured in Free Lance-Star newspaper article

Carey featured in Free Lance-Star newspaper article

CHAPTER 3

When The Good You Do, Don't Do You No Good

I retained John Mell as my counsel to represent me from the *Law Offices of Mell & Frost* in Fredericksburg, VA. As a result of the Coronavirus pandemic that swept the nation my court date was constantly delayed. Two years would pass before my case was eventually set for trial.

In the months leading up to trial my attorney engaged in plea bargaining with Stephanie Fitzgerald, the Assistant Commonwealth's Attorney. Plea bargaining is negotiations in a criminal procedure between the defendant's attorney and the prosecutor in which the defendant agrees to plead "guilty" or "no contest" in return for the reduction of the severity of the charges. I was willing to accept responsibility and therefore never intended to argue guilt or innocence. I merely asked for a reasonable sentence based on mitigating circumstances including the fact that in this isolated incident there were no injuries, I possessed a valid driver's license, and the vehicle was insured.

We also offered multiple letters in support of my character and contributions to the local community. We asked that the Felony Leaving the Scene of an Accident and the Felony Child Abuse/Neglect charges be reduced to misdemeanors in hopes that the lesser offenses would not violate my probation. Mrs. Fitzgerald advised that she'd agree to reduce the felonies to misdemeanors in exchange for me also pleading guilty to a charge of DUI which would be upgraded from reckless driving. I was confused as to why she'd suggest I plead guilty to an offense that I wasn't originally charged with nor was there any evidence of, given I wasn't arrested until days after the accident. In addition to the upgraded charge, she informed us that she would also be pursuing an active time of incarceration relative to that in my sentencing guidelines if I had been convicted of the felony.

Sentencing guidelines are formed to provide sentence recommendations based on historical practices using information regarding the nature of the current offense(s) and a defendant's criminal history. A probation officer adds up all the points on the guidelines worksheet to get a total score. Using the overall rating, the officer will use a grid to convert the total score to the recommended guidelines sentencing range. These guidelines are the framework for judges' sentencing decisions. The problem with this method is that more points are given for a defendants' prior convictions opposed to the circumstances of the current offense. Therefore, those with a background tend to receive much harsher sentences compared to an offender facing the same charge but no previous record.

I was reluctant to take the plea as are most facing prosecution. Due to the "Trial Penalty" 97% of defendants accept plea offers leaving less than 3% choosing to go to trial in state and federal cases.[8] The Trial Penalty is the substantial difference between the sentence offered in a plea prior to trial versus the sentence a defendant receives after a trial. This penalty is now so severe and pervasive that it has virtually eliminated the constitutional right to a trial by jury. To avoid penalty, one must surrender many fundamental rights essential to a fair justice system.

I believed that in examining the totality of the circumstances a Circuit Court Judge may be more lenient when sentencing me but feared the consequences I'd face if I opted to go to trial – my assumption was wrong. I reasoned that the plea offered was excessive and a result of sentencing guidelines reflecting choices made by me as a young man in my early twenties and not the redefined man I had grown to become. I felt that such a lengthy incarceration would only prove to be punitive in nature and not rehabilitative. I feared it would be detrimental to all that I'd worked so hard to accomplish since my release from prison both personally and professionally.

I had been on bond and under the supervision of Senior Probation and Parole Officer, Chavioleyette

Mitchell for two years since the original offense date. During that time, I had not committed any new infractions, maintained compliance, consistently tested negative for illegal substances and accomplished case planning goals. I felt that my crime and character did not indicate a likelihood of repetition and that public interest didn't require that I be imprisoned. I considered myself a good social risk and that an alternative sentence where I could continue serving the community would be more appropriate.

Despite my apprehensions to accepting the offer, my biggest fear about going to trial was the possibility of being convicted of a felony charge and thus violating my probation. In the criminal justice system, probation allows convicted defendants to be released with a suspended sentence for a specified duration during good behavior. If the probationer violates a condition of probation the court may revoke any portion of

> **December 8 - 28**
> Middlesex County Sheriff Guy L. Abbott reported that the sheriff's office documented 636 calls for service between December 8-28, 2008. The following are a list of felony arrests made in that period as well as some of the incidents reported:
> Spencer Antoine Carey, 25, of Fredericksburg was arrested on Dec. 8 at a home on Box Elder Arch in Virginia Beach. Virginia Beach Police were alerted to Carey's suspected whereabouts in its city by way of a teletype message previously sent by the Middlesex Sheriff's Office. Carey was arrested on two outstanding Middlesex County warrants that charged him with attempted second-degree murder and use of a firearm in the commission of a felony. A total of four felony charges have been brought against Carey as the result of a firearm being discharged inside a home during a party on McKans Road in Jamaica on Aug. 23. The investigation of the events that transpired at the residence was headed up by Investigator C.B. Sibley.

a previously suspended sentence and order the probationer to serve a term of imprisonment.

I had been on indefinite probation since 2005 when I was convicted of my original felony charges in Gloucester County, VA for Possession with intent to

distribute Schedule I or II and Possession of a firearm while in Possession of Schedule I or II. I was also on probation in Middlesex County, VA for an incident in 2008 when I was convicted of Possession of a firearm by a non-violent felon and an Attempted Unlawful wounding. Additionally, I was also on probation for Distribution of Schedule I or II in 2008 in Essex County, VA.

> **SHERIFF'S REPORT**
> **GLOUCESTER**
> The following felony crime was recently reported by the Gloucester Sheriff's Office:
> A traffic stop for defective equipment around 1 a.m. Saturday led to the arrest of two persons and the seizure of approximately six ounces of powder cocaine with a value of $16,800, according to Capt. Darrell Warren of the Sheriff's Office.
> Warren said the investigator who made the stop smelled marijuana as he approached the vehicle. He said a subsequent search of the car and its occupants found 3.5 grams of cocaine on one suspect, one ounce of marijuana in some clothing allegedly belonging to the other suspect and a loaded .45 caliber handgun in the front floorboard. In a search of the trunk, Warren said officers found 5.5 ounces of cocaine tucked behind some upholstery along with two loaded 12 gauge shotguns and digital scales.
> Arrested were and Spencer Antoine Cary, 22, of Norfolk. Each was charged with possessing a controlled substance classified in Schedule I or II with the intent to manufacture, sell, give or distribute and possessing a pistol, shotgun, rifle or other firearm while committing or attempting to commit the illegal manufacture, sale, distribution or the possession with the with the intent to manufacture, sell or distribute a controlled substance classified in Schedule I or II of the Drug Control Act or more than one pound of marijuana. In addition, Cary was charged with misdemeanor marijuana possession. Each was held without bond.

Since my release from incarceration in February 2014 I had violated my probation once before in September of that same year when I was convicted of a Driving Under the Influence (DUI) charge in Spotsylvania County, VA. The DUI was a misdemeanor and I received 5 days in jail. However, the new conviction violated the conditions of my probation in Essex, Middlesex, and Gloucester. Ultimately, I'd receive 30 extra days in jail from each of those three jurisdictions. I'd also receive three additional felony convictions because in Virginia any new conviction even a misdemeanor violates felony probation and is thus also a felony. Yes, you read that correctly! For a misdemeanor DUI that I received 5 days in jail it resulted in an additional 3 felony convictions and 90 days in jail because it violated my probation. Needless to say, the thought of rejecting the plea offer and risk violating probation with a felony conviction given my experience of violating with a misdemeanor was terrifying.

The negotiations concluded with me agreeing to plead guilty to Misdemeanor Leaving the Scene of an Accident and an Alford plea to Misdemeanor DUI and Misdemeanor Contributing to the Delinquency of a Minor. An Alford plea is not an admission of guilt but it acknowledges that the evidence is sufficient for a conviction. In Virginia, misdemeanors are punishable by up to 12 months in jail. The plea offer required the Judge to sentence me to the maximum of 12 months on all 3 charges for a total sentence of 36 months. Contingent upon mitigating circumstances to be presented at trial the agreement prevented the Judge from suspending more than 12 months of the sentence.

CHAPTER 4

The More Things Change, The More They Remain The Same

The Commonwealth of Virginia vs. Spencer Carey (CR19001571, CR19001572, CR19001826) was held in the Circuit Court of the County of Spotsylvania on April 15, 2021 and was presided over by the Honorable William E. Glover, Judge. Below is an excerpt of the Judge's ruling

```
 1  April 15, 2021
 2                      NOTE: Court convenes at 9:00 a.m.
 3          This case is called to be heard at 12:06 p.m.
 4          The Court Reporter was first duly sworn. This is
 5          an EXCERPT of the Judge's ruling ONLY as follows:
 6                  THE COURT: Well, Mr. Carey, a
 7          couple of things. You're a fortunate man, which
 8          is an odd thing to say to somebody who's signed a
 9          plea agreement that's going to resolve in them
10          going to jail. But you're fortunate because of
11          the people that came here today, people who had
12          faith in you and still do and it's not the usual
13          case because the witnesses who wrote letters for
14          you and the witnesses who testified for you
15          today, are not people who are doing that because
16          they're your friends. These are people who know
17          what they're talking about.
18                  DEFENDANT CAREY: Thank you, Your
19          Honor.
20                  THE COURT: And there's nothing
21          that I can say to you that will be more eloquent
```

FRANCES K. HALEY & ASSOCIATES, Court Reporters
10687 Spotsylvania Avenue, Fredericksburg, VA 22408
Phone: (540) 898-1527   FAX: (540) 898-6154

than what Ms. Shank said from the stand. You let those people down and, yet, you heard the rest of what she said. She believes that you are the person today that she believes you were before you had this collision and left the scene and she's going to believe that when you are back in your school teaching people to cut hair and beards. That's not -- when I say it's good fortune, that makes it sound like it's luck. It's not. You earned that.

DEFENDANT CAREY: Thank you.

THE COURT: I also really do understand what you said about the fear that you had about losing everything. You are the product of a system that I consider to be profoundly unfair. I found myself, Mr. Carey, scratching my head thinking why would Mr. Mell, who is both very experience but also careful about what he does, why would he -- why would he have you agree to this agreement? But I understand that the circumstances for that are created by things that are in your life in the past and the Commonwealth understands it too.

If I thought, Mr. Carey, that you were being taken advantage of by the Commonwealth, I would have rejected the plea agreement. But, I think, that the plea agreement in this case is intended to be a compromise, a compromise that acknowledges things that neither you nor Mr. Mell, nor the Commonwealth in this county, nor I, have the ability to change, not in your case. There are things that are changing about the way people are subject to being re-incarcerated and re-incarcerated and re-incarcerated.

Those things are changing, but in your case, you committed offenses that require punishment and when you say you take responsibility, you know that in a way probably better than any of us who haven't served a jail sentence, a prison sentence. It's -- I'm very reluctant to send you to jail, but I understand the circumstances that you're dealing with and I'm without the power and is Ms. Fitzgerald and Mr. Mell to change that.

It's called comfort, I'm sure, Mr. Carey, but I will tell you that I share the confidence that your witnesses have that you'll be back. I will not insult you by saying that everything is going to be okay because that's not true, but the things that you have accomplished since you were released from prison, are extraordinarily unusual for people that are in this courtroom.

I initially intended to say something to you about not trusting the barber that shaves his head, but in all honesty, you're going to be back and you're going to serve the community that you live in.

So pursuant to the terms of the plea agreement, on each of the three charges, you're sentenced to twelve months and on each charge, four months is suspended, so you have

```
twenty four months to serve, which is what the
contract says. The contract prohibits me from
making any other specific provisions with respect
to that, at least at this point, Mr. Carey.
```

As you can tell from the record, Judge Glover acknowledged the dilemma with which I was being faced. A problem that he, himself being one of the highest-ranking officials in our local judicial government, a Circuit Court Judge could not save me from. This crisis plagues many not only in the judicial system but in all other areas of life. In spite of my best efforts to not allow my past to define me nor dictate my future, in spite of my best efforts to rehabilitate and redefine myself, in spite of all my efforts to desist and detach; the harsh reality is I could never outlive my past.

Judge Glover called me a "fortunate man," stating, *"...the things that you [I] have accomplished since you [I] were released from prison, are extraordinarily unusual for people that are in this courtroom."* He sympathized with the fear I had of losing everything I had worked so hard to attain. He articulated in his own words that I was the *"product of a system that he considered to be profoundly unfair,"* even questioning why my attorney would advise me to accept such an agreement. He even expressed his confidence in my continued service to the community upon my release. Nonetheless, even amidst his reluctance to send me to jail, Judge Glover succeeded that the *"circumstances that I'm dealing with, circumstances that are created by things that are in my life in the past"* are *"things that neither you [I] nor Mr. Mell, nor the Commonwealth in this county, nor I, have the ability to change."*

Ultimately, I was sentenced pursuant to the terms of the plea agreement. I received 12 months with four months suspended for each of the three misdemeanors leaving me with a 24-month sentence. In Virginia, offenders are only required to serve 50% of a misdemeanor sentence contingent upon good behavior. The judge remanded me to the custody of the Rappahannock Regional Jail in Stafford, Virginia with a release date of April 15th 2022; exactly one year to the day.

Weeks later I would be called to intake at the jail and served with two felony warrants from Gloucester and Middlesex counties for violating my probation. Luckily, my probation time in Essex County had expired. I retained Michael T Soberick, Esquire from the Law Offices of

Dusewicz & Soberick to represent me in both jurisdictions. Ironically, my trial dates for Gloucester and Middlesex were set for June 15th and June 16th respectively in the neighboring counties with the same Circuit Court Judge hearing both cases.

The Commonwealth of Virginia vs. Spencer Antoine Carey (CR05000455-03, CR05000456-03) was held in the Circuit Court of the County of Gloucester on June 15, 2021 and was presided over by the Honorable Jefferey W. Shaw, Judge. The counsel on behalf of the Commonwealth was William J. Wittenbrook, Assistant Commonwealth's Attorney. Below is an excerpt from the trial's transcript.

```
17            MR. SOBERICK: Judge, that's all of our
18    evidence.
19            THE COURT: All right. Mr. Wittenbrook,
20    anything you would like to say?
21            MR. WITTENBROOK: Your Honor, I can tell the
22    Court it's not every day that we see somebody who has a
23    history like Mr. Carey has. He has the letters that
24    he's provided to this Court and the transcripts that
25    he's provided to this Court from his last hearing and a
```

woman who is no longer his wife who is testifying on his behalf. I would submit to the Court that our role here is to do justice and to love mercy and I think that Mr. Carey, from all accounts, even from the Major Violation Report, he was downgraded to Shadowtrack. He had been doing well. I believe he made a mistake. I understand this Court suspended a significant portion of his sentence last time and basically gave him time served. I will tell the Court that from what I've read and what I've seen here today, it doesn't appear that the Mr. Carey that's before the Court today is the same Mr. Carey that was before the Court the last time. And whatever sentence the Court fashions, I would just ask the Court to take into account that we are to do justice and to love mercy. Mr. Carey sounds like he's been a productive member of society since he's been released. He has opened a barbershop. He's not only being a thriving member of the community in that way by having revenue coming in but he's also trying to teach other people that skill and trying to keep other people from making the same mistakes that he made. It's not every day that I stand up here as a prosecutor basically giving a defense argument, but from everything that I've seen, I don't think it would be in the state's interest to punish him any more than what the Court would -- would be inclined to punish him that's basically what has happened to him in the other jurisdiction, Judge. I think that Mr. Carey would be a good example to the community and I would hate to see him -- I would hate to see everything that he had worked for completely ruined because he made a mistake out of fear one night.

THE COURT: Mr. Soberick.

MR. SOBERICK: Judge, I think everybody agrees, including Judge Glover in Fredericksburg, Mr. Carey is a rehabilitated person. Probation and everything that he's been through has been successful with Mr. Carey. I mean he's made mistakes and he's made -- he's done something that he shouldn't have done. But the situation in Suffolk that we're here for is a situation where he wanted to have his son with him at this event, where he was giving out food and games and his son was running it and participating and he was doing a good thing in the community but he didn't bring the child back like he should have on Sunday. He brought the child back on Monday. The Judge gave him a $100 fine and suspended it. You've read the transcript from the Spotsylvania hearing, Judge. Clearly that Judge was at least torn as far as what he was doing. He ultimately went along with the plea agreement but he was clearly torn.

Judge, he's rehabilitated. He's not the same guy that was driving around in 2005 with drugs and money and gun in the trunk of his car. That was a young student at Norfolk State at the time. He's not that person anymore, Judge. He has gone in the right direction. He hasn't upped the ante. He has turned himself around. He has become a productive member of society. As Judge Glover pointed out, these are letters not from friends. These are people that don't know him as a friend. They know him professionally and they say wonderful things about him. Judge, he's earned the right. I would ask the Court to consider suspending any sentence that the Court may impose. He's serving a two-year sentence in Stafford County for misdemeanors. Admittedly he'll be out in a year but that year is still not going to run until April of 2022, so he still has time behind bars. If the Court is inclined to give him any sentence, Judge, I would ask that you run it concurrent with the current sentence and not exceed what he will be serving. Thank you.

THE COURT: Mr. Wittenbrook, anything further?

MR. WITTENBROOK: No, Your Honor.

```
 1            THE COURT:  Mr. Carey, the Court finds you
 2   violated the terms of your probation and suspended
 3   sentence.  I'm now ready to sentence you.  Is there
 4   anything you would like to say before I sentence you or
 5   is there any reason I should not sentence you today?
 6            THE DEFENDANT:  No, Your Honor.  I'm just
 7   asking for the mercy of the Court.
 8            THE COURT:  All right, sir, I revoke -- on
 9   case number 05-455 I revoke the 13 years and 9 months
10   previously suspended.  I resuspend 13 years and
11   6 months of that sentence for a period of 1 year on
12   conditions I'll give you in a moment.
13            On case number 05-456 I revoke the 5 years
14   previously suspended.  I resuspend all of that for a
15   period of 1 year.
```

Mr. Wittenbrook expressed to the court, *"It's not every day that we see somebody who has a history like Mr. Carey,"* and *"It's not every day that I stand up here as a prosecutor basically giving a defense argument."* He recognized my transformation, saying, *"It doesn't appear that the Mr. Carey that's before the Court today is the same Mr. Carey that was before the Court the last time,"* and *"Mr. Carey sounds like he's been a productive member of society since he's been released."* Mr. Wittenbrook asserted that he *"didn't think it would be in the state's interest to punish me anymore."* In his own words he stated, *"I think Mr. Carey would be a good example to the community and I would hate to see him – I would hate to see everything that he had worked for completely ruined because he made a mistake out of fear one night."* Most importantly, Mr. Wittenbrook, being an Assistant Commonwealth's Attorney of Virginia would offer that which I've never heard before and that was to remind the court that its *"role here is to do justice and to love mercy."* Ultimately, Judge Shaw would revoke 18 years 9 months and re-suspend 18 years and 6 months leaving 3 months for me to serve in addition to my sentence in Spotsylvania. The following day I would face him yet again this time in the Circuit Court of the County of Middlesex. Judge Shaw would revoke 3 years of my previously suspended sentence and re-suspend 2 years and 9 months leaving 3 months to serve which he would run concurrent with the Gloucester County sentence.

CHAPTER 5

If It Don't Cost You Anything, It's Not Worth Anything

I was returned to Rappahannock Regional Jail (RRJ) in Stafford, Virginia where I was to serve my 24 month sentence before being transferred to Gloucester County Jail to complete the additional three months. Incarceration in itself is a dehumanizing experience. Re-incarceration, however, would prove to be much more traumatic. The already dire conditions at RRJ were further heightened by the coronavirus pandemic. Due to overcrowding, I was the third man housed in a two-man cell. I was forced to sleep on the floor. I slept beside the toilet where my only escape was to cover myself with a blanket while my cellmates defecated within arm's reach. This is also where I was served my breakfast, lunch, and dinner. Additionally, the facility was plagued with security issues as a result of staff shortages. To inmates this equated to continuous administrative lockdowns that restricted us to our cells for twenty-three hours or more at a time for months.

In spite of the physical conditions endured it failed in comparison to the mental anguish suffered. In the documentary, *Fade in Full*, I likened being incarcerated to being buried alive where you're forced to deal with yourself. My thoughts flashed back to 2008 when I was entering prison as *"College Boy"* with a release date of

March 26, 2021. I remembered having to leave my daughter Aniya Ayanna Carey a second time and accept the fact that I'd miss the first eleven years of my son's life. I searched for comfort in vowing I'd be released in time for their more influential years. My heart broke with the reality that here I was absent from their world yet again. I had to accept that I was no longer the *"College Boy"* in his mid-twenties but rather a nearly forty-year-old Antoine still bound by the circumstances of my former self.

    I was ashamed as I sat amongst the younger generation knowing I was old enough to be their father yet unable to save them from the wasted years of incarceration that lay ahead. I was saddened by the harsh reality of recidivism and how despite their best efforts to remain free the majority of the inmates, like myself, we're returning once again. I had prided myself on being a voice for the voiceless and here I was once again amongst the voiceless. I had accepted every invitation to go inside the facilities to speak with the inmates and here I was once again amongst the inmates. A part of me died inside as I saw myself within each of them and rightfully so as we all shared the same experience.

    Antoine Carey the man and *Faded & Co.* the brand are both merely a culmination of past experiences. Without these experiences Antoine is just a man and *Faded & Co.* is just another business. It's the willingness to share these experiences that has allowed me to connect with people around me and to foster positive relationships within the community. The sharing of these experiences has inspired others while giving them hope in the midst of their own hardships. My aim has never been more than to share my story. I've shared my unadulterated truth as I've lived it and witnessed first-hand and not just something someone told me. Each experience has caused me sleepless nights, tears shed, and time spent away from my loved ones that I can never get back. A wise man once told me that if it doesn't cost you anything then it's not worth anything. Conversely, if it has cost me something then it must be something of value. It's for this reason I've chosen to continue sharing my story.

CHAPTER 6

He Who Is Closest To The Problem Is Closest To The Solution

As mentioned in the foreword, my aim has only been to share my story. The sharing of my experiences has been just as therapeutic to me as it has been beneficial to those I've shared my story with. I've never claimed to have all the answers nor to present myself as anything more than I am. On the contrary, I've consistently stated the opposite. Too often when people are recognized and highlighted for any level of success, they take on this stigma of perfection and are held to a higher standard. I've always been afraid of such a responsibility for fear of failing everyone. I know and accept that I'm only Antoine. I'm a work in progress and strive every day to be the best version of me. I realize where I've grown and where I'm in need of growth. This not only keeps me humble it also keeps me relatable.

Unfortunately, my story has kept me in close proximity to the criminal justice system and its issue of mass incarceration. According to the *Institute for Crime & Justice Policy Research,* the U.S has the highest incarceration rate in the world; with every single state incarcerating more people per capita than any independent democracy on Earth.[1] While the United States accounts for only 5% of the world's population it's responsible for 20% of the world's incarcerated.[2] There are currently over 2 million people in the nations' prisons and jails which is a

500% increase over the past 40 years.[1] In fact, if the incarceration rate remains unchanged 1 out of every 20 U.S. residents can expect to serve time in prison in their lifetime.[5]

Additionally, the average cost per person in prison ranges from about $14,000 to $70,000 per year depending on the state.[7] In 2019 the state expenditures on corrections were $56.6 billion.[3] To add insult to injury, the National Institute of Justice reports that almost 44% of criminals released return before their first year out of prison with 77% returning within 5 years.[4] What's most disheartening is that there is still no evidence that the increased incarceration rate correlates to a decrease in the crime rate.

The age-old appendage says, *"If it ain't broke don't fix it."* The Honorable Judge Glover called it, " a system that I (he) consider to be profoundly unfair." In my honest, admittedly biased opinion I feel the system is extremely flawed and yet is operating exactly as it was intended to work. Regardless of what you choose to call it the facts remain the same.

According to Virginia Performs, which examines juvenile and adult recidivism: The ability to re-enter society with viable options for self-sufficiency is a telling factor in recidivism, especially among adults. No matter how rehabilitated they are upon release, ex-offenders typically have few resources and often experience difficulty finding housing, reliable transportation, jobs or help. The stigma attached to being an ex-offender is a major employment barrier; many are also unprepared for the world of work, lacking educational attainment, vocational training and life skills. Frustrated by those challenges, many return to their former social circles - and to illegal activities.[6]

    I think we can all agree that given the complexity of this issue there is no single remedy. In my opinion once an individual has been exposed to incarceration something is lost that can never be regained nor unlived. I feel that after this happens there is no win and one can only salvage that which remains. The best solution is to be preventative rather than reactive. Nonetheless, once affected we must endeavor to minimize the negative effects of incarceration and help to restore these people to a useful place in society.

    The Honorable Judge Glover stated, *"There are things that are changing about the way people are subject to being reincarcerated and reincarcerated and reincarcerated."* Needless to say, there's plenty more work to be done. Given my story and present circumstances I feel the sentencing guidelines should be reconstructed to give more consideration to the current offense as opposed to prior convictions. I would not suggest eliminating the guidelines completely as I understand that an offender's background does tell a story; just not the whole story. Except in cases of repeat offenses individuals should not be held accountable for "debts to society" that have already been paid. JUSTICE IS FOR ALL, that includes the offender!

Secondly, I feel that sentences should be rehabilitative versus punitive in nature. Incarceration is not always effective nor a benefit to the community. Each individual and the circumstances surrounding their offense are unique and should be reflected in their sentence. Alternative sentences assess the risk relative to reoffending and address the root causes of criminal behavior. These alternatives should be utilized to provide rehabilitation thus protecting the public by preventing future crimes. One such example is the Right Roads Program offered by FailSafe-Era that includes coaching, counseling and mentoring. Alternative sentencing options would in turn reduce the incarceration rate as well as the cost of housing those convicted.

Lastly and most importantly I believe the answer to this problem as is most of society's ills is found once all involved parties are brought together for dialogue. This happens when everyone affected is represented and allowed to share their perspective based on their experience. The sharing of these experiences individually and collectively builds relationships and thus a sense of community. Once the community as whole is involved, change is then initiated and eventually accomplished. It's with that I encourage everyone to share their story and thank you all for allowing me to continue sharing mine.

CHAPTER 7
Many Hands Make Light Work

Incarceration affects us all. Many organizations have been formed to combat recidivism and to make the transition back into society as seamless as possible. If you or anyone you may know has been affected by incarceration, I encourage you to utilize all resources made available. Listed below are a few organizations I've been blessed to partner with that may be able to provide that which you stand in need of. Feel free to contact them for assistance.

1. **AFOI** *(Assisting Families of Inmates)* provides opportunities for regular, meaningful visitation, referrals to community resources, and other services that help families cope with incarceration and prepare for release and reunification

    1 North 5th Street
    Suite 416
    Richmond, VA 23219
    (804) 643-2401
    Website: https://afoi.org/

2. **FailSafe-ERA** provides reentry support and services to the residents of Fredericksburg, Spotsylvania, Stafford, Caroline, and King George Communities.
    10304 Spotsylvania Avenue,
    Suite 100
    Fredericksburg, VA 22408
    Phone: (540) 479-3021
    Website: https://www.failsafe-era.org/
3. **Families Against Mandatory Minimums** *(FAMM)* is an American nonprofit advocacy organization founded in 1991 to challenge mandatory sentencing laws and advocate for criminal justice reform.
    1100 H Street NW, Suite 1000 | Washington, D.C. 20005
    Phone: (202) 822-6700
    Website: https://famm.org
4. **Micah Ecumenical Ministries** is a Christ-centered community supporting people experiencing chronic homelessness and identifying pathways to sustainable housing.
    1013 Princess Anne St.
    Fredericksburg VA 22401
    Phone: 540-479-4116
    Website: https://micahfredericksburg.org/

5. **Northern Neck Regional Jail Reentry & Transition Services** provides post-incarceration services to clients residing in the Counties of: Essex, Lancaster, Northumberland, Richmond County, and Westmoreland

    P.O. Box 1090

    Warsaw, VA 22572

    Phone: (804) 333-6006

6. **OAR of Richmond, Inc.** *(Offender Aid and Restoration of Richmond)* - enhances public safety by providing individuals and families affected by incarceration with transition services that support safe and successful reintegration into the community.

    3111 West Clay Street

    Richmond, VA, 23230

Phone: (804) 643-2746

    Website: http://www.oarric.org/

7. **Thurman Brisben Center** is a homeless shelter with transformative services for sustainable housing and resolution of poverty.

    471 Central Rd

    Fredericksburg, VA 22401

    Phone: (540) 899-9853

    Website: https://brisbencenter.org/

References

1 Data source: https://www.prisonpolicy.org/global/2021.html; Institute for Crime & Justice Policy Research

2 Data source: https://www.sentencingproject.org/criminal-justice-fact; Institute for Crime & Justice Policy Research

3 Data source: https://www.sentencingproject.org/wp-content/uploads/2021/05/state-expenditures.png; National Association of State Budget Officer

4 Data Source: National Institute of Justice - https://nij.ojp.gov/topics/articles/measuring-recidivism#statistics; Bureau of Justice Statistics, Recidivism of State Prisoners - Released in 2005 data collection, 2005–2014

5 Data Source: U.S. Department of Justice - https://bjs.ojp.gov/content/pub/pdf/Llgsfp.pdf

6 Data Source: https://vaperforms.virginia.gov/

7 Data Source: https://www.vera.org/publications/price-of-prisons-2015-state-spending-trends/price-of-prisons-2015-state-spending-trends/price-of-prisons-2015-state-spending-trends-prison-spending

8 Data Source: https://www.nacdl.org/Document/TrialPenaltySixthAmendmentRighttoTrialNearExtinct

About The Author

Antoine Carey is a local entrepreneur and public speaker who was once incarcerated. He decided not to let his past define him nor dictate his future. He obtained his barber's license while in prison and now is the owner of Faded & Co. Barbershop and Faded & Co. Barber Academy located in Fredericksburg, VA. Carey feels it's his moral obligation to share his story in an effort to combat recidivism and help break generational cycles of incarceration. He debuted a documentary on his life, Fade in Full "The Story of Antoine Carey" in 2019. He accepts his social responsibility to utilize every opportunity afforded to give back to and influence the community. Carey endeavors to continue sharing his story via "From Whom Much Is Given…." with an aim of restoring hope in the lives of those affected by incarceration and to be a voice for the voiceless.